M000043670

Everything's
Going to Be
Okay

Edited by
Douglas Pagels

Blue Mountain Press™
Boulder, Colorado

We gratefully acknowledge the permission granted by the following authors, publishers, and authors' representatives to reprint poems or excerpts from their publications: Susan Polis Schutz for "In my own particular case..." from DEPRESSION AND BACK. Copyright © 2010 by Stephen Schutz and Susan Polis Schutz. All rights reserved. Disney•Hyperion, an imprint of Disney Book Group LLC, for "Sometimes things just fall apart" and "Time heals all wounds..." from THE WINNING ATTITUDE! by Michelle Kwan. Copyright © 1999 by Michelle Kwan Corp. Reprinted by permission. All rights reserved. Charles Higgins for "How do we put our life back together?" from GRACE. Copyright © 2005 by Charles Higgins. All rights reserved. Grand Central Publishing for "Just keep putting one foot..." and "People who care about you..." by Stacey Halprin and "By accepting that you are in control..." by Dr. Jane Greer from WINNING AFTER LOSING by Stacey Halprin, Foreword by Dr. Jane Greer. Copyright © 2007 by Stacey Halprin. Reprinted by permission of Grand Central Publishing. All rights reserved. And for "Each and every one of you..." from TEN THINGS I WISH I'D KNOWN BEFORE I WENT OUT INTO THE REAL WORLD by Maria Shriver. Copyright © 2000 by Maria Shriver. Reprinted by permission of Grand Central Publishing. All rights reserved. Faith Words for "Every journey has to start somewhere..." from KNIT TOGETHER by Debbie Macomber. Copyright © 2007 by Debbie Macomber, Inc. Reprinted by permission of Faith Words. All rights reserved. And for "The future begins with..." and "You must make a decision..." from YOUR BEST LIFE NOW by Joel Osteen. Copyright © 2004 by Joel Osteen Publishing. Reprinted by permission of Faith Words. All rights reserved. Cader Books for "When you start a new trail..." by Ruby Bridges, "Katharine Hepburn once told me..." by Martina Navratilova, and "Be able to pick yourself up..." by Mario Andretti from THE MOST IMPORTANT THINGS I KNOW, compiled by Lorne A. Adrain. Copyright © 1997 by Lorne A. Adrain. All rights reserved.

Acknowledgments are continued on the last page.

Library of Congress Control Number: 2010904939
ISBN: 978-1-59842-525-3

▌ and Blue Mountain Press are registered in U.S. Patent and Trademark Office.
Certain trademarks are used under license.

Printed in China.
First Printing: 2010

♲ This book is printed on recycled paper.

This book is printed on paper that has been specially produced to be acid free (neutral pH) and contains no groundwood or unbleached pulp. It conforms with the requirements of the American National Standards Institute, Inc., so as to ensure that this book will last and be enjoyed by future generations.

Blue Mountain Arts, Inc.
P.O. Box 4549, Boulder, Colorado 80306

Contents

(Authors listed in order of first appearance)

Douglas Pagels

Michelle Kwan

Charles Higgins

Stacey Halprin

Debbie Macomber

Ruby Bridges

Sherwin T. Wine

Marcus Aurelius

Pamela Vaull Starr

Melody Beattie

Dr. Jane Greer

Lisa Taylor

Taylor Hicks

Joel Osteen

Ashleigh Brilliant

Robin Crow

Joan Anderson

Patti LaBelle

Suzanne Somers

Kathy Lee Gifford

Malcolm Boyd

Kim Klaver

Suzy Toronto

Julia A. Boyd

Amy Grant

Eileen Fisher

Montel Williams

Peg Neuhauser

Ken Burns

Robert Half

Christopher Robin

Joyce Meyer

George P. Burnham

Alyssa Milano

Jim Rohn

Anne Guisewite

Randy Pausch

Patch Adams, MD

Martina Navratilova

Katharine Hepburn

Darcy Lewis

Kathy Ireland

Valerie Harper

Dave Barry

Mario Andretti

Morrie Schwartz

Cindy Horyza

Rokelle Lerner

Sister Alice Potts

Alex Rodriguez

Tanya Tucker

Susan Polis Schutz

Christopher Reeve

Harold S. Kushner

Thomas Edison

Lucille Ball

Mary Alice Williams

Mickey Walker

Ali MacGraw

Jeanette Osias

Kermit the Frog

Ted Williams

John Burroughs

Robin Roberts

Piper Perabo

O. S. Marden

Diana Ross

Carol Tuttle

Rachael Ray

Hugh Prather

Sadie Delany

J. Hartley Manner

Derek Jameson

Breena Clarke

Charles M. Schwab

Eleanor Roosevelt

Maria Shriver

Cheryl Richardson

Letty Cottin Pogrebin

Chérie Carter-Scott

Alicia Keys

Words to Help You Get Through a Difficult Time

I know this is a difficult time. I'm sorry that things are so uncertain right now. In the days ahead, I know that you will stay as strong as you need to be... to see your way through.

I know that you will discover more courage and hope and faith inside you than you ever knew you had. I know your prayers will help to light your way if you ever get lost. I know that things will get better, day by day, and that the passage of time has a wonderful way of turning things around.

And I know that you can do every positive thing it takes to make it through any difficult time because... that's what remarkable people do. And one of those very special people, without a doubt... will always be you.

:: Douglas Pagels

Sometimes things just fall apart.

:: Michelle Kwan

How do we put our life back together?
What comes first?

:: Charles Higgins

Just keep putting one foot in front
of another.

:: Stacey Halprin

Just Breathe, Believe, and Begin

Every journey has to start somewhere, and believing in yourself is the first step toward achieving your purpose. Once you believe you can do it, your mind automatically starts figuring out how it can be done.

Debbie Macomber

When you start a new trail equipped with courage, strength, and conviction, the only thing that can stop you is you!

Ruby Bridges

$\mathcal{I}$ believe that the strength to cope with a crazy world comes from within ourselves, from the undiscovered power we have to look reality in the face and to go on living.

Sherwin T. Wine

$\mathcal{V}$ery little is needed to make a happy life. It is all within yourself, in your way of thinking.

Marcus Aurelius

$\mathcal{R}$each high, for stars lie hidden in your soul. Dream deep, for every dream precedes the goal.

Pamela Vaull Starr

There is magic in setting goals. Things happen. Things change. I accomplish important projects. I change. I meet new people. I find myself in interesting places. I make it through difficult times with a minimum of chaos. Problems get solved....

Goals give us direction and purpose. I don't get into my car, turn on the ignition, start driving, and hope I get someplace. I decide where I want to go, then I steer the car in that general direction. That is how I try to live my life, too.

:: Melody Beattie

By accepting that you are in control and by staying in the driver's seat with both hands on the wheel, you can learn to make smart decisions, take the right turns, and keep moving forward in your life.

:: Dr. Jane Greer

The Choice Is Yours

The future is ours to channel in the direction we want to go.

:: Lisa Taylor

Forward is the only direction that leads to a better place.

:: Taylor Hicks

The future begins with what happens in your life today. As we make the most of the present moment, we build our future one day at a time.

:: Joel Osteen

I try to take one day at a time, but sometimes several days attack me at once.

:: Ashleigh Brilliant

Right Here, Right Now

Remember, our life is a reflection of our attitudes. With a positive attitude you will create positive results.

:: Robin Crow

My new attitude is captured in a sentiment of Goethe's that is inscribed on a mug I sip my coffee from each morning: "Nothing is worth more than this day." My life changed when I learned to concentrate on little moments. It is during the little moments rather than the big ones that I learn the most. Little moments contain all the wisdom, all the truth, all the pleasures that I need to continue to grow.

:: Joan Anderson

We must live in the moment. It is all we really have. The past is gone and the future may never come. If we spend all our time dwelling on yesterday or worrying about tomorrow, we lose all the joy and sweetness of today.

:: Patti LaBelle

I don't know what tomorrow will bring, but today I am aware that forgiveness heals, that blame is wasted energy, that awareness of each moment of life is precious. I don't want to waste any of it. I want to be present, in the moment, and accept all that happens to me as the gift that it is and to grow and evolve into the best person I can be.

:: Suzanne Somers

Each day is a gift. That's why it's called the present.

Unwrap it.

:: Kathy Lee Gifford

When at First You Don't Succeed...

At precisely the same moment when there is apparently nothing we can do about anything, that's the time to move into action. Devise a strategy. Make a plan. Call a meeting. Adopt Plan B. Find an alternative.

Malcolm Boyd

Do you have a Plan B?

A Plan B? You know, that back-up plan in case whatever you're doing now doesn't pan out?...

It might be the Plan B you suddenly need to create "out of thin air" because something drastic and unexpected happened to your Plan A.

Kim Klaver

$\mathcal{P}$lan A is always my first choice. You know, the one where everything works out to be happily ever after. But more often than not, I find myself dealing with the upside-down, inside-out version where nothing goes as it should.

It's at this point that the real test of my character comes in. Do I sink or do I swim? The choice is all mine.

Life is all about how you handle Plan B.

Suzy Toronto

$\mathcal{I}$'m all for Plan B's, even C's and D's. I think that's why God made the alphabet. So that every time something goes askew in our lives, we can always make a new plan, twenty-six times if we have to.

Kathy Lee Gifford

The Healing Process

Sometimes our hurts can be so strong and painful that it's difficult to imagine our survival, but we do survive and we do go on. With each new day we move toward a place of healing the pain we've suffered. I'm not talking about forgetting, because we may never forget what caused our hurt. But with time we do have the power to emotionally move away from whatever it was that hurt us. If you give yourself nothing else, please give yourself all the time you need to heal.

:: Julia A. Boyd

Grief has its own timetable.... The time it takes to heal is the time it takes.

:: Amy Grant

You may have to go through pain, but on the other side is the good stuff.

::Eileen Fisher

If you're like me, on some days you'll find that Living Well is a real challenge.

But there will be other days when you'll do it perfectly — and it will be much easier than you think. I know you're going to feel better than you felt before you started, and that's the thing that will motivate you to keep going and keep succeeding.

Keep taking small steps, making small improvements, and savoring small victories.

If you stick with this, the rewards are incalculably huge....

The power is in your hands.

::Montel Williams

Stay Strong...

Remember the old Timex watch commercials on television? "Takes a licking and keeps on ticking" was the message. The watches were put through all kinds of dramatic punishments, but in the end those watches were still ticking....

What about the people who endure tough times with courage and grace, or bounce back from crises with renewed energy when logic tells you the situation should have left them depleted and discouraged? For all the talk about burnout, the fact is that the majority of people spend most of their lives coping amazingly well. We are far more resilient and skilled at surviving and thriving than we give ourselves credit for.

▪▪ Peg Neuhauser

$\mathcal{P}$ersevere. Life is tough and requires hard work and determination in all things.

::Ken Burns

$\mathcal{P}$ersistence is what makes the impossible possible, the possible likely, and the likely definite.

::Robert Half

$\mathcal{P}$romise me you'll always remember: you're braver than you believe, and stronger than you seem, and smarter than you think.

::Christopher Robin to Winnie the Pooh

Do you ever feel like giving up? Perhaps you're discouraged about your finances or you're facing problems with your health, your marriage, or your children. Sometimes problems seem so overwhelming that the road ahead seems too steep to climb.

We all go through these times. I've wanted to give up and quit many times through the years. But when I realized I had nothing interesting to go back to, I determined to keep pressing on.

Even though continuing to move forward is sometimes painful, it is far better than giving up.

Joyce Meyer

"I can't do it" never accomplished anything; "I will try" has performed wonders.

George P. Burnham

...and Continue On

Life for me is about getting up and going to work, about putting myself out there and having people tell me thanks but no thanks. It's about trying and failing, and trying and failing, and trying and failing some more, until you don't fail, until bliss descends upon those who have not given up.

Alyssa Milano

How long should you try? Until.

Jim Rohn

$\mathcal{K}$nowing that you *should* move forward and committing that you *will* move forward makes all the difference.

■■ Robin Crow

$\mathcal{H}$ow you feel is your own choice. Things don't do you in. You do yourself in. You can choose to be happy or miserable — whichever you prefer. Your attitude makes the difference. If a calamity strikes, you can sift through the rubble to see what new opportunity it may open up for you. Or you can choose numerous negative responses, including going crazy which, unfortunately, some people do....

You'll know you're on the right track when you feel at peace with yourself, no matter how displeased someone else may be about it. That's their problem. Yours is to stay on course following your own star.

■■ Anne Guisewite

Bounce Back

As I see it, there's a decision we all have to make, and it seems perfectly captured in the Winnie-the-Pooh characters created by A.A. Milne. Each of us must decide: Am I a fun-loving Tigger or am I a sad-sack Eeyore? Pick a camp. I think it's clear where I stand on the great Tigger/Eeyore debate...

I won't let go of the Tigger inside me. I just can't see the upside in becoming Eeyore.

■■ Randy Pausch

Be happy. I refer not to a moment of joy during one of life's peak experiences but to a basic pattern of enduring happiness. It takes no greater effort to be happy every day than to be miserable.

Each of us chooses the background hues of his or her own portrait. A person can choose to be happy.

■■ Patch Adams, MD

Katharine Hepburn once told me,
"It's not what you do in life, it's what
you finish!" But many people don't even
start, because they are afraid of failure.
To me the only failure is when you don't
even try. So set your path, be brave, do
your best and *smile*, because you are
doing all of the above.

:: Martina Navratilova

Don't moan. Don't complain.
Think positively.

:: Katharine Hepburn

With a hula hoop in your soul and an
ongoing sense of humor in your being,
you can cope.

:: Darcy Lewis

Keep Smiling
Through It All

As long as I have more laugh lines
than frown wrinkles, I'm happy.

:: Kathy Ireland

Wrinkles should be a sign of having lived,
having put in some time and put out a ton
of energy. Creases, lines, age spots, sags
should be badges of honor for having stayed
in the game of life and participating full-out.
We need to appreciate the time put in on
the planet by the owner of a face with such
obviously earned credits....

A face full of experience, knowledge, humor,
and peace.

:: Valerie Harper

$\mathcal{I}$ believe that all of us truly need teaching on this subject of how to enjoy where we are on the way to where we are going.

Joyce Meyer

$\mathcal{E}$njoy life! Hold on to your dreams, and never let them go. Show the rest of the world how wonderful you are! Give circumstances a chance, and give others the benefit of the doubt. Wish on a star that shines in your sky. Take on your problems one by one and work things out. Rely on all the strength you have inside. Let loose the sparkle and spirit that you sometimes try to hide. Stay in touch with those who touch your life with love. Look on the bright side and don't let adversity keep you from winning. Be yourself, because you are filled with special qualities that have brought you this far, and that will always see you through. Keep your spirits up. Make your heart happy, and let it reflect on everything you do!

Douglas Pagels

Sometimes You Just Have to Laugh

Time heals all wounds. Laughing can heal a few wounds too.

Michelle Kwan

Never stop laughing.

Dave Barry

Be able to pick yourself up and brush yourself off every day. While life is not always fair, it is manageable. It is a matter of attitude and confidence.

Mario Andretti

...and Sometimes You Just Need to Cry

"Ah, Mitch, I'm gonna loosen you up. One day I'm gonna show you it's okay to cry."

Morrie Schwartz to Mitch Albom

People are so afraid that if they start to cry they won't quit. Trust me, no one has ever died of crying. Flowers need lots of water to bloom and sometimes we do, too.

Cindy Horyza

My tears carry the old hurts from deep inside, coursing up until they spill over, pouring out, flowing freely. I feel the pain and hurt leaving my body as the tears wash away the misery and tension I have carried for so long.

Rokelle Lerner

We've been raised in a culture that denies us the value of experiencing our sadness. I believe that tears are a sign of release. Crying is a way of letting go, moving forward out of the dark recesses of our pain and grief. Have you ever noticed how much better you feel after a good cry? Tears are a natural part of our emotional cleansing system and they promote our ability to heal.

:: Julia A. Boyd

God didn't give you tear ducts for nothing.

:: Sister Alice Potts

No matter what, we all need support —
family members, friends, and other adults.
Don't be afraid to talk with someone if
you are hurting inside.

:: Alex Rodriguez

People who care about you want to help you
just as much as you want to help the people
you care about. So don't cheat them out of
the chance to do something good for you
when you really need it.

:: Stacey Halprin

If we want the support of others we have to
be willing to ask for it. True, asking will make
us vulnerable, but at least we've done our part.
I've discovered others are often willing to be
supportive when they're given a chance.

:: Julia A. Boyd

You Don't Have to Go Through This Alone

My family and friends wanted me to talk to a professional about my state of mind, but I balked. I still couldn't get past thinking that seeking help was a sign of weakness.... I also didn't quite understand that depression is nothing to be embarrassed about or ashamed of. It's something that happens to people, and something that they can work through. But they usually can't do it alone.

:: Tanya Tucker

In my own particular case, the support I received from my family, therapist, and friends was invaluable to my recovery.

I now look forward to most days and appreciate life's beauty. I'm passionate about music, people, and nature the way I used to be. I'm dancing again.

:: Susan Polis Schutz

Keep the Light of Hope Alive

At some time, often when we least expect it, we all have to face overwhelming challenges. We are more troubled than we have ever been before; we may doubt that we have what it takes to endure. It is very tempting to give up, yet we have to find the will to keep going. But even when we discover what motivates us, we realize that we can't go the distance alone.

When the unthinkable happens, the lighthouse is hope. Once we find it, we must cling to it with absolute determination.... Hope must be as real, and built on the same solid foundation, as a lighthouse; in that way it is different from optimism or wishful thinking. When we have hope, we discover powers within ourselves we may have never known — the power to make sacrifices, to endure, to heal, and to love. Once we choose hope, everything is possible. We are all on this sea together. But the lighthouse is always there, ready to show us the way home.

Christopher Reeve

There will be dark days, days of loss and days of failure, but they will not last forever. The light will always return to chase away the darkness, the sun will always come out again after the rain, and the human spirit will always rise above.

Harold S. Kushner

It seems like some things weren't meant to be, and some plans just weren't supposed to work out. There will always be losses and disappointments to deal with. But we're given the gift of a new sunrise each morning... and a new chance for things to get better every single day.

Let life show you new ways of doing things and different ways of making your dreams come true. Keep your hopes up and remind yourself that moving on may not always be easy, but... it's really not that hard. Let every experience help you grow wiser and become stronger. And don't ever forget: you've got what it takes to make it through. Just keep the light alive. And keep believing... in you.

Douglas Pagels

Be a Doer

If we did all the things we are capable of doing, we would literally astound ourselves.

Thomas Edison

Making our dreams come true can be hard. Sometimes it's not until we find ourselves completely desperate, with everything on the line, that we're willing to do something about it. Sometimes it comes down to taking that leap of faith and going for broke. Sometimes we just have to *jump*....

Don't be afraid to follow your heart. If you're willing to jump, your net will appear.

Robin Crow

I don't think you should ever run away from who you are. Rather, I think you should run toward whomever you want to be.

Taylor Hicks

Be a Dreamer

All of you should be working around the clock, every day for the rest of your life, fulfilling your dreams. Not because you're paid to do it, but because you can't help it. It feels that good.

Patch Adams, MD

Remember that so much happiness comes to dreamers and believers. Dreams are like stories... where anything is possible. You can guide the pen along the page and write whatever your heart desires. Dreams are deep, meaningful feelings spoken in a language all their own. Dreams are hard to interpret into words, but they are easy to translate into smiles. Dreams are directions to the paths you'll walk someday. Dreams are compasses that show the way. Dreams are destinations on the journey of your life.

I want you to keep believing in your dreams... and learn how to do what it takes to make them a reality.

Douglas Pagels

Life Is One Big Learning Curve

One of the things I learned the hard way was that it doesn't pay to get discouraged.

:: Lucille Ball

I am learning every day that you can't change the painful past. You can't fix it or forget it or wish it away. But you can come to accept it and use it as an opportunity to change yourself in a way that gives you strength and serenity and happiness....

I am learning that taking the risk of trusting and feeling and actually talking about it isn't as frightening as it sounds. That it's human to suffer losses, give them a name, grieve them, and go on. That you always have someplace to turn.

:: Mary Alice Williams

You learn in life there are always the ups and downs. We must have enough sense to enjoy our ups and enough heart to get through our downs.

:: Mickey Walker

I have learned from the lean times that there is absolutely nothing as paralyzing as a warped reverie about the past or some projected terror of the future. Slowly I am learning that as long as I stay focused on the right-now, I am fine.

:: Ali MacGraw

Right now my life is just one learning experience after another. By the end of the week I should be a genius.

:: Jeanette Osias

Step One: Survive

There are two ways to react to bad things. The easy way is to get angry, cast aspersions, and generally get in a bad mood about the world and everything in it.... The other way to react takes a lot more work. You can get over it. That's right; accept it, be happy you survived it, and get past it....

We are often at our best when we're facing our worst situations. Know that when you come out of it, you can be a better you.

Kermit the Frog

Just keep going. Everybody gets better if they keep at it.

Ted Williams

Step Two: Thrive

As you sit reading this book someone is climbing Mt. Everest, a couple is sailing around the world in a sailboat, a woman is skydiving for the first time. They are all pushing against their comfort zone, becoming stronger, more confident, and less afraid. Climbing mountains and crossing oceans are big accomplishments, but every time we push ourselves, even with little tasks and small steps, we grow stronger.

It may sound like a cliché, but there is nothing more inspiring than the power of the human spirit. Even when it seems like we're not going to make it another step, that spirit survives. There are no limits to how high the human spirit can soar.

Robin Crow

Dance Lessons

No matter where you are in life, if you can make a few key changes, you can make a huge difference in your whole world.

:: Montel Williams

In life, the only thing that is certain is change. Change is a given. Change is expanding and contracting. We must learn to meet, embrace, and dance with change. It is something we're always going to face.

:: Kathy Ireland

Difficulties arise in the lives of us all. What is most important is dealing with the hard times, coping with the changes, and getting through to the other side where the sun is still shining just for you.

It takes a strong person to deal with tough times and difficult choices. But you are a strong person. It takes courage. But you possess the inner courage to see you through. It takes being an active participant in your life. But you are in the driver's seat, and you can determine the direction you want tomorrow to go in.

Hang in there... and take care to see that you don't lose sight of the one thing that is constant, beautiful, and true: everything will be fine — and it will turn out that way because of the special kind of person you are.

So... beginning today and lasting a lifetime through... hang in there, and don't be afraid to feel like the morning sun is shining... just for you.

⠿ Douglas Pagels

Soothe Your Soul

Here in Maine, alone and quiet, I am in touch with a kind of sanity I have been missing. I need silence in which to absorb the colors of twilight — the mauve shadows of the trees at sunset, and the great clusters of smoky clouds as they gather overhead. I need stillness to appreciate the curls of woodsmoke as they come out of the central chimney. And I need time to note each separate layer of color in the moss-agate landscape of pine and birch.

And when I have done that, I feel centered again. The big challenge will be how to duplicate the serenity I find here when I am in an environment that lacks the nourishment of this one.

Ali MacGraw

You are always nearer the divine and the true sources of your power than you think... Every place is under the stars, every place is the center of the world.

:: John Burroughs

Finding beauty in the world around us is so important for alleviating the frustrations of daily life. "Getting away" to lovely places restores our energies. We surround ourselves by beauty and rediscover our hope.

:: Sherwin T. Wine

Listening In

We all have an inner voice, and sometimes we ignore it, or it gets drowned out by all the noise of life.... If you sit quietly and listen, you can hear it. And your inner voice will tell you what will really make you happy and fulfilled — what is truly in your heart. I have found it crucial in times of self-doubt to listen to that voice.

:: Robin Roberts

It's a noisy world and the answer inside you sometimes has trouble being heard. But take the time to quietly listen and you'll never go wrong.

:: Piper Perabo

Looking Ahead

$\mathcal{I}$ know a smiling old lady who... looks forward toward the coming day as she would toward a journey she was taking, and she is always expecting some new delight, some wonderful experience. She says that the very thought that the day holds beautiful things in store for those who expect them... has been a constant inspiration. It has helped to bring her the very things she expects.

O. S. Marden

$\mathcal{T}$omorrow is a beautiful road that will take you right where you want to go... if you spend today walking away from worry and moving toward serenity... and leaving behind conflict and traveling toward solutions.

If you can do what works for you, your present will be happier and your path will be smoother. And best of all? You'll be taking a step into a beautiful future.

Douglas Pagels

A New Day Beckons

I know that whatever is making me feel bad is not going to last forever unless I allow it to. Tomorrow will be better.

Diana Ross

In every moment, during every day of your life you have choices. The choice to create more struggle, or the choice to create more freedom and joy. Choose thoughts that support you in feeling good more and more each day.

It will take practice to gain mastery over your thoughts and feelings. Never give up. Never settle for mediocrity. You can accomplish more than you think.

Carol Tuttle

Periods of greatest growth in our life often come during pain and sadness. We have to call everything into question. We must decide how to go on.

Such moments are so strong that, in a curious way, they affect the course of our whole life. We learn so much, so fast. Momentarily we're overwhelmed, thrown for a loop, unable to move. Sorrow invades our life. We look for resources to deal with it.

We absorb the pain, gradually place sorrow behind us, and gently resume the pace of living. Life beckons with vitality and colors and new risks. But we're not the same, will never be the same again. We've been shaken. We were wounded. Now we are in a healing process. Having come up against a mighty force, we've survived. We are stronger now than we were before. Our life is richer.

Malcolm Boyd

Sweet Advice

God gives everyone the ingredients
to a good, happy life. It's up to us
to make the most of them.

:: Rachael Ray

There is a time to let things happen
and a time to make things happen.

:: Hugh Prather

Life is too good to waste a day. It's
up to you to make it sweet.

:: Sadie Delany

My recipe for happiness... is simply looking forward.

:: J. Hartley Manner

My recipe for success: to be absolutely sure what it is you want to do... and then go for it with total dedication and enthusiasm.

:: Derek Jameson

You should be cooking on all four burners.

:: Breena Clarke

The difference between getting somewhere and getting nowhere is the courage to make a... start.

:: Charles M. Schwab

You must make a decision that you are going to move on. It won't happen automatically. You will have to rise up and say, "I don't care how hard this is, I am not going to let this get the best of me."

:: Joel Osteen

You gain strength, courage, and confidence by every experience in which you really stop to look fear in the face. You are able to say to yourself, "I have lived through this... I can take the next thing that comes along." You must do the thing you think you cannot do.

:: Eleanor Roosevelt

You Can Do This

Each and every one of you is an awesome, powerful, resilient human being capable of living the life you design for yourself. It's within you to carve out your own future, create your own destiny. You're in a glorious moment, filled with possibility. Try to keep this feeling of endless possibility alive as long as possible. Whenever you feel it fading, call it back and renew it. That's a gift you can give yourself. You deserve to feel great about your life.

:: Maria Shriver

Happiness on the Horizon

As your life starts to change and the magic starts to happen, people may call you lucky.... The truth is, anyone can be lucky if they're willing to do the work. Get started now! The life you were meant to live is waiting.

:: Cheryl Richardson

The time has come for me to change.

I can and I am: it is exciting work, brand-new territory.

:: Ali MacGraw

Though no one can make a brand-new start, anyone can start from now and make a brand-new end.

:: Anonymous

$\mathcal{I}$ can see everything from here: where I've been and what I've left behind; where I'm going and who I wish to be. I've named my fears and overcome a few, swallowed my regrets, focused on what to cherish and what to change, and tried to accept the things I cannot help.

▪   ▪   ▪

What I wish for myself and for all of us is to feel until the very end of life that each day is a gift of time and possibility.

▪▪ Letty Cottin Pogrebin

Celebrate the fact that you made it through the dark times and are on your way to a new future.

:: Chérie Carter-Scott

I made it. The journey, and the revelations it brought me, have changed me forever. I'm no longer that scared, shy, insecure little girl who didn't see her worth or her blessings. It took me a long time to understand that so much of my pain was about me. Me not listening to my heart. Me needing others to love me because I didn't love myself. Me holding on in fear instead of letting go in faith. Me not living for today because I was worrying about tomorrow. Me blocking the blessings.

All that is passed... there's a brand-new me. Unafraid. Unbroken.

:: Patti LaBelle

Everything's Going to Be Okay

I have experienced all these things.... I want to share this now because I have learned from them, I have suffered through them, I have grown from them, and now I'm more aware of myself as a woman and as a person who goes through the things that cause life to be experienced in all its crazy, upside-down-sideways-inside-out-glory. I am more aware of what I feel and how to deal and where to go from here.

:: Alicia Keys

Just go out there and do what you need to do.

:: Anonymous

If You Do These Ten Things...

you will be able to see your way through just about anything

■ Stay positive! (Hopeful people are happier people.) ■ Choose wisely. (Good choices will come back to bless you.) ■ Remember what matters. (The present moment. The good people in it. Hopes and dreams and feelings.)

■ Don't stress out over things you can't control. (Just don't.) ■ Count every blessing. (Even the little ones add up to a lot.) ■ Be good to your body. (It's the only one you get...)

■ Listen to the wishes of your heart. (It always seems to know what's true, what's right, what to do, and where to go with your life.)

■ Understand how special you are! ■ Realize how strong you can be. ■ And know that, YES, you're going to make it through, no matter what.

Maybe you won't be dancing in the streets or jumping on the bed... but you are going to get through the day, the night, and each and every moment that lies ahead. (I promise.)

■■ Douglas Pagels

Acknowledgments continued...

We gratefully acknowledge the permission granted by the following authors, publishers, and authors' representatives to reprint poems or excerpts from their publications: The International Institute for Secular Humanistic Judaism–North American Section for "I believe that the strength…" and "Finding beauty in the world…" from STAYING SANE IN A CRAZY WORLD by Sherwin T. Wine. Copyright © 1995 by Sherwin T. Wine. All rights reserved. HarperCollins Publishers for "Life for me is about getting up…" from SAFE AT HOME by Alyssa Milano. Copyright © 2009 by Alyssa Milano. All rights reserved. And for "Wrinkles should be a…" from TODAY I AM A MA'AM AND OTHER MUSINGS ON LIFE, BEAUTY, AND GROWING OLDER by Valerie Harper. Copyright © 2001 by Valerie Harper. All rights reserved. And for "I am learning every day…" by Mary Alice Williams from QUIET TRIUMPHS by Mary Alice Williams. Copyright © 1999 by Mary Alice Williams. All rights reserved. And for "My recipe for…" by Derek Jameson and "Being armed with…" by David Gee from THE RELAXATION LETTERS, compiled by Audrey Burns Ross. Copyright © 1993 by Audrey Burns Ross. All rights reserved. And for "You gain strength, courage…" from YOU LEARN BY LIVING by Eleanor Roosevelt. Copyright © 1960 by Eleanor Roosevelt. Copyright renewed 1988 by Franklin A. Roosevelt. All rights reserved. Hazelden Foundation, Center City, MN, for "There is magic in setting…" from GRATITUDE: CONFIRMING THE GOOD THINGS IN LIFE by Melody Beattie. Copyright © 1992 by Hazelden Foundation. All rights reserved. Crown Publishers, a division of Random House, Inc., for "Forward is the only direction…" and "I don't think you should…" from HEART FULL OF SOUL by Taylor Hicks and David Wild. Copyright © 2007 by Taylor Hicks, LLC. All rights reserved. And for "I don't know what tomorrow…" from AFTER THE FALL by Suzanne Somers. Copyright © 1998 by Suzanne Somers. All rights reserved. Brilliant Enterprises for "I try to take one day…" from I TRY TO TAKE ONE DAY AT A TIME, BUT SOMETIMES SEVERAL DAYS ATTACK ME AT ONCE by Ashleigh Brilliant. Copyright © 1987 by Ashleigh Brilliant. All rights reserved. Robin Crow for "Remember, our life is…," "Knowing that you *should*…," "Making our dreams come true…," and "As you sit reading…" from JUMP AND THE NET WILL APPEAR. Copyright © 2002 by Robin Crow. All rights reserved. Broadway Books, a division of Random House, Inc., for "My new attitude is…" from A WEEKEND TO CHANGE YOUR LIFE by Joan Anderson. Copyright © 2006 by Joan Anderson. All rights reserved. And for "You may have to go through pain…" by Eileen Fisher and "You should be cooking…" by Breena Clarke from WHAT I KNOW NOW: LETTERS TO MY YOUNGER SELF, edited by Ellyn Spragins. Copyright © 2006 by Ellyn Spragins. All rights reserved. And for "As your life starts to change…" from TAKE TIME FOR YOUR LIFE by Cheryl Richardson. Copyright © 1999 by Cheryl Richardson. All rights reserved. And for "Celebrate the fact that…" from IF SUCCESS IS A GAME, THESE ARE THE RULES by Chérie Carter-Scott. Copyright © 2000 by Chérie Carter-Scott. All rights reserved. Riverhead Books, an imprint of Penguin Group (USA), Inc., for "We must live in the moment" and "I made it" from DON'T BLOCK THE BLESSINGS by Patti LaBelle and Laura B. Randolph. Copyright © 1996 by Patti LaBelle. All rights reserved. Ballantine Books, a division of Random House, Inc., for "Each day is a gift" and "I'm all for Plan B's…" from JUST WHEN I THOUGHT I'D DROPPED MY LAST EGG by Kathy Lee Gifford. Copyright © 2009 by Kathy Lee Gifford. All rights reserved. Malcolm Boyd for "At precisely the same moment…" and "Periods of greatest growth…" from RICH WITH YEARS. Copyright © 1994 by Malcolm Boyd. All rights reserved. Kim Klaver for "Do you have a Plan B?" from DO YOU HAVE A PLAN B? Copyright © 2002 by Kim Klaver Max Out Productions, Inc. All rights reserved. Suzy Toronto for "Plan A is always my first choice." Copyright © 2009 by Suzy Toronto. All rights reserved. Julia A. Boyd for "Sometimes our hurts can…," "We've been raised in a culture…," and "If we want support…" from GIRLFRIEND TO GIRLFRIEND. Copyright © 1999 by Julia A. Boyd. All rights reserved. Doubleday, a division of Random House, Inc., for "Grief has its own timetable…" from MOSAIC: PIECES OF MY LIFE SO FAR by Amy Grant. Copyright © 2007 by Amy Grant. All rights reserved. And for "As long as I have more laughs…" and "In life, the only thing…" from POWERFUL INSPIRATIONS: EIGHT LESSONS THAT WILL CHANGE YOUR LIFE by Kathy Ireland and Laura Morton. Copyright © 2002 by Kathy Ireland WorldWide Inc. And for "'Ah, Mitch, I'm gonna loosen you up" by Morrie Schwartz from TUESDAYS WITH MORRIE by Mitch Albom. Copyright © 1997 by Mitch Albom. All rights reserved. Dutton Signet, a division of Penguin Group (USA), Inc., for "If you're like me…" and "No matter where you are…" from LIVING WELL by Montel Williams. Copyright © 2008 by Mountain Moves, Inc. All rights reserved. John Wiley & Sons, Inc., for "Remember the old Timex watch…" from I SHOULD BE BURNT OUT BY NOW… SO HOW COME I'M NOT? by Peg Neuhauser. Copyright © 2004 by Peg Neuhauser. All rights reserved. Running Press, a division of Perseus Books, Inc., for "Persevere. Life is tough…" by Ken Burns, "Never stop laughing" by Dave Barry, and "Just listen to your heart" by Piper Perabo from WISDOM TO GROW ON by Charles J. Acquisto. Copyright © 2006 by Charles Acquisto. All rights reserved. Excerpts from DISNEY'S POOH'S GRAND ADVENTURE: THE SEARCH FOR CHRISTOPHER ROBIN by Kathy Henderson published by Mouse Works are © Disney Enterprises, Inc. and are used by permission.